]

MW01169363

Rejection To Connection!

A Practical and Spiritual
Guide to Accessing

Freedom and Deliverance
from Rejection

Contact Prophetess Tyson at
www.prophetessyolandadtyson.com

Prophetess Yolanda D. Tyson

From Rejection to Connection!

Contact Prophetess Tyson at
www.prophetessyolandadtyson.com

Contact Prophetess Tyson at
www.prophetessyolandadtyson.com

A

A Practical Guide to Accessing Freedom and Deliverance from Rejection

Prophetess Yolanda D. Tyson

Contact Prophetess Tyson at
www.prophetessyolandadtyson.com

ISBN

Contact Prophetess Tyson at
www.prophetessyolandadtyson.com

Disclaimer

This book in no way intends to provide therapeutic information or intervention. It does not replace the valid and often necessary therapeutic work of a professional therapist or counselor. It is provided with the understanding that the author and publisher in no way are providing legal, financial or psychological advice. The reader, in so doing, agrees to take full responsibility for their well-being and safety in engaging with this material. The author and publisher specifically disclaim any liability for the use or application of the contents of this book.

Contact Prophetess Tyson at
www.prophetessyolandadtyson.com

This book is dedicated to my Lord and Savior, Jesus Christ

and to all who supported me in prayer as I wrote this book.

It is also dedicated to my beloved mother who has gone home

to be with the Lord, to my father whom I love so dearly,

And to my #1 cheerleader.

Contact Prophetess Tyson at
www.prophetessyolandadtyson.com

TABLE OF CONTENTS

Introduction

Chapter 1
The Unwanted Child

Chapter 2
Where does Rejection Come From?

Chapter 3
The Rejected Personality

Chapter 4
What Does the Bible Say About
Rejection
and Your True Identity?

Chapter 5
How to Overcome the Spirit of
Rejection

Contact Prophetess Tyson at
www.prophetessyolandadtyson.com

Introduction

For the purposes of our conversation, it is important that we have a common understanding of the definition of rejection, particularly from a spiritual perspective.

The principality of Rejection is an evil spirit that rules over a multitude of other evil spirits. This collective of spirits operate as the armor of Rejection with the specific assignment of Rejection. They want to reject others. They want to feel rejected. They will do whatever they can to be rejected; To rob people of relationships through rejection; To make people feel that others don't love them through rejection; To make people feel worthless through rejection.

Rejection means to cast away from one; to throw away; to refuse; to put aside. As a noun, the word rejection means a person or thing rejected as though not up to some standard. So rejection means to back-throw, to remove from your presence, to throw off. It is a form of unbelief, saying that you are not accepted by God, or by anyone else including yourself, and in order to be accepted by God you have to be accepted by men first. Rejection sets man as your god. It declares that validation

10

of who you are and who you are not rests on a human who accepts you or does not accept you.

Rejection communicates that a person is unacceptable, of no value, doesn't belong, is unwanted, can't fit in and is unloved. This message is communicated through a disgusted look, disdain, an impatient answer, a snub, or through neglect or abandonment, and even through silence.

Studies show that a baby in utero knows whether it is wanted or not, even recognizing the voice of its parents. Thomas Verney in his book *The Secret Life of the Unborn Child* confirms that there is active life in the womb. His research indicates:

- Unborn babies hear, taste, feel and learn in the womb.

- Womb experiences shape a child's attitude and expectations about himself.

- Deep persistent patterns of feelings in the mother affect the unborn child.

- A father's feelings about his wife and the unborn child also affect the pregnancy.

- If the womb is friendly, a baby may be predisposed to good health, happiness and normal development; if the womb is unfriendly, the baby may be predisposed to ill health, nervousness, irritability, and arrested development

While in the womb, unborn children may absorb a variety of wounding experiences. In their spirits they may react with defensiveness, resentment, aggression, distrust or withdrawal and grow into adulthood expressing attitudes still lodged in their hearts. This may result from:

- Conception out of wedlock, conception in anger, rape, incest or adultery, or conception in a drug-dependent relationship

- Mother had miscarriage or abortion before this conception

- Threatening illness of mother or fetus, mother anorexic or bulimic (fear of gaining weight)

- Coming at a wrong time in the parents' lives (marital difficulties, poverty, inconvenience)

- Being the "wrong sex"

- Experiencing intense emotions from the mother (fear, anger, rejection, verbal abuse, etc.) or fighting in the home environment

- A difficult birthing experience (breech birth, cord wrapped around the neck, unusually painful delivery, caesarean birth, induced labor, baby early or late in coming, etc.)

- Being released for adoption or parents who considered adoption

- Attempted or failed abortion of fetus

- Death of father or abandonment by one or both parents

12

In these instances, a child may react wrongly to the wounding forming false judgment and, later in life, reap the consequences of sin in the womb.

A child conceived in anger, rape, incest, adultery, in a drug-dependent relationship or out-of-wedlock may sense early in its prenatal development that its very existence is a cause of stress or anxiety to its mother. (This curse can bring poverty in every area of life and can go back 10 generations – Deut 23:2) Unfortunately, this may be the beginning of worry, rejection, low self-esteem, and fear of abandonment.

Often parents who are married conceive at inopportune times, such as too soon after marriage, before finishing college, too close to another child, mother's fear of the birth process, conceived late in life, or maybe at a time of strain on the family budget. Babies can sense these anxieties. Some people are told by their parents that they would never have had them if abortion had been legal. Even when babies are planned or wanted, a person may still need prayer, for example, if the mother suffered a previous abortion or miscarriage or severe sickness, accident or tremendous grief during pregnancy.

Sound has an impact on the unborn. Children can also pick up on any anger, quarrel, yelling or screaming between mother and father and then can harbor that anger or resentment for a lifetime.

Even traumatic birthing can have an effect on the unborn. Long labor, breech births, instrumental assistance, umbilical cords wrapped around necks, premature or c-section deliveries, Rh blood factor problems, death of the mother during birth, placement in an incubator or immediate surgery, abortion or attempted abortion all can contribute to traumatic experiences that lead to emotional or spiritual issues in later life.

13

Our experiences are stored from the very beginning of our creation and we begin to build up responses, judgments, attitudes, and expectations from them. Not all children with similar womb experiences react in the same way. God-given temperament and grace can intervene.

God brought us into this world. He breathed life into us. He chose us, planned us and called us by our name. If God did not breathe life into us, we would simply be a sex act. We are not a mistake of nature or a biological accident. Father God called us according to His purpose and glory.

In all this woundedness, Jesus' redeeming power can reach back into those early birth experiences and bring light to darkness, wholeness to incompleteness and restoration to the inner person. He can change attitudes and wrong reactions. Lives are turned around because the light of His love chases out the darkness in souls. "The lamp of the Lord searches the spirit of a man; it searches out his inmost being." (Proverbs 20:27)

WHY I WROTE THIS BOOK

When the Lord told me to write this work about rejection, I immediately knew that it would be one of the most challenging undertakings of my life.

Let me tell you why.

To talk to you about rejection meant that there were things I had to face about my own rejection. And to be honest, I wasn't really looking forward to that. I knew there would be healing for me on the other side, but I really didn't feel like I

14

was up to the task of what I might have to go through to get there.

Which may be where you are now too. I get it.

You may also be in the other place I was.

In one word...demoralized. That one word sums up what seems like my whole experience, including depression, despair, and discouragement.

What I knew for a fact was that life couldn't keep looking like it was. No joy. No peace. No prosperity. No power. All there seemed to be was struggle, struggle, strife and more struggle all from the root source of rejection as God was revealing it to me. The only place I was even remotely happy was in the pulpit, preaching and prophesying under the Holy Ghost anointing. Once the anointing lifted, I was left with my life again. What I came to understand was that if life outside of the pulpit was going to be different it had to start with me being different first. I had to want to be delivered from the root of rejection and all its effects. I had to first desire healing, at any cost, in order to allow God to heal me. And that is the same decision you must make right now. Continue to be right in your own truth or choose to allow the ultimate Truth of God to heal your life.

Please know, beyond a shadow of a doubt, that it is possible to be healed, and I mean completely healed, from the bitterness of rejection. I am a living witness that God is able to perform that which He promised. And if you are reading this, you are under the anointed prayer of healing that covers this work. No matter when, no matter where, I am standing with and for you that you surrender to the Healing Power of the Holy Ghost that infuses this work and receive the fullness of His blessed healing.

15

Pray this prayer out loud before you go any further. Ask God hear you as you pray with sincerity.

"Lord, I come to you in a space of repenting from every unrighteous thought and every unrighteous deed. Father please forgive me, in Jesus' name. Now Father please close every door that was opened giving the devil legal access to my mind, my body and my spirit, in Jesus' name. I give you all praise, all honor and all glory as I come humbly before You now. I am asking You to open the gates of my eyes, my ears, my heart, and my understanding. I am seeking Your Word of Truth concerning me. Help me to see who I am to You. Help me to accept Your Truth as my own. I desire to be made free from the bondage of rejection in all its forms and that starts right now as I read these words. Thank You. In the name of Jesus, I believe it is so. Amen."

This just set the atmosphere for your deliverance to be successful. Let us now proceed.

Contact Prophetess Tyson at
www.prophetessyolandadtyson.com

Chapter 1

The Unwanted Child

My mother cried when she found out that I existed. She had not wanted children from anyone other than her first husband. My father denied me. He thought he couldn't have children. The results of this for me was the creation of a womb experience of rejection that has colored my life in some way most of my life.

One would think that my life would be one of great joy and satisfaction since I became my mother's favorite child and my father's only child. And the truth of it is that there was a certain level of privilege that I enjoyed.

Daddy was always eager to spend time with me even after the divorce. He was always on time to pick me up and absolutely spoiled me with affection, attention, money and virtually anything my little heart desired. As a teen, my allowance was $100 a week and all I had to do for it was smile. No heavy lifting, no chores, no worries. At 14, I drove to my driver's education classes, much to the dismay and disapproval of the instructor. He pitched a fit every day he'd see me

17

wheeling up to the course site, yelling himself red in the face for me to get out of the car. I was the envy of all of my friends.

I truly was the apple of my daddy's eye, as they say. His eyes weren't big enough to take me in with the love he feels for me. My dad is almost seven feet tall, built like a linebacker. I just barely break five feet. One of my greatest thrills in life was when he would put me on his shoulders! Talk about being on top of the world! I could stay there forever! I felt safe, loved, chosen, and oh, so special. There was truly nothing like it!

My mother could never get enough of me either. I was her world. She made sure I had the best education money could buy, which at that time was through a Catholic private school. She bought me designer clothes, shoes, everything. I had the complete Holly Hobby bedroom set from comforter to curtains. Whatever I wanted, within reason, I got.

Mother kept me grounded too. She taught me how to share and be considerate of others. I gave half of my clothes to a young lady I went to school with who had a lot of brothers and sisters. Mother bought school clothes for her when she bought clothes for me. Half of whatever she intended to spend on me was spent on her clothes. I learned early that to give is divine.

Mother was a powerful Woman of God. She was the first to believe in the call on my life to the ministry. She had seen it first hand on many occasions. Even as a child, instead of playing house, I played "church." My cousins sat on the pews, which were the stairs, while I preached the Word of God to them. They repented and turn their lives around during "services." I laid hands on them and they would cry over their sins. In my teens, I and some other youth at the church were playing around before service started. I was preaching to them

18

and telling them they needed to be saved and accept Christ as their Savior. In the midst of this "playing around," the Holy Ghost fell and they were all slain in the Spirit and began to speak in tongues. When everyone arrived for the actual service, they joined in and church started right then and there with us! So when I started my church, Mother was my first member. She was the first Church Mother. She was my armor bearer and my "road dog." Mother traveled with me as I evangelized across the country. She raised funds for the church. She helped build the church. She was my number one fan.

While she was no light weight with the discipline, she clearly favored me over my sisters and brother who are much older than I am. My oldest sister is of an age to possibly be my mother. Right. Can you say, "change of life baby?" That was another reason my mother was less than excited about being pregnant with me. Like most women in their 40's who have already given birth to several children, three girls and a boy before me, she thought she was finished with all of that "birthin' babies" stuff. Though I'm sure it wasn't until she was in her elder years that she was flat out, straight up, unashamed about her preference for me. I'm positive the message came across loud and clear somehow to my siblings in our youth. My sister was jealous of me because I was our mom's proclaimed favorite. She intentionally pushed me down a flight of stairs to get rid of me when I was little. I suppose that spoke volumes at the time. It was probably the first time the enemy tried to kill me. For the most part, I grew up an only child given the ages of my siblings. They weren't around much. They moved out of the house as soon as they were able. Given that much distance, it makes sense that we weren't close.

I'm not sure that there was anything conscious about my decision to turn to the streets in my teens. By then, around age 7 or 8, I had already been sexually abused by my "play uncle" and a strong sense of rejection had set in.

19

He told me that if I told my mother, he would have to kill her and if I told my father, daddy would kill him. It would all be my fault, he said. Often, sexual abuse victims become overly responsible for the lives and well-being of others. It comes from these kinds of experiences. When the abuser is familiar to the victim, they take advantage of the child's need for safety and love and their need for their family to be safe. They play on these vulnerabilities for their own safety and personal gain.

Studies also show that sexual abuse causes the victim to feel like an object, their very personhood challenged and denied. They are not seen or related to as a person by the abuser. They are instead considered to be a thing at their disposal. This is how the abuser, in their mind, can take advantage of a child. Ironically, much of the information out there about child sexual abuse speaks to the control that an abuser feels over their target. They develop trust first, taking advantage of the familiarity and relationship. Secrecy provides another aspect of weaponry against the child. For a child, having a secret is one of the most powerful weapons in the abuser's arsenal. According to the Abuse Watch website (www.abusewatch.net)

"The 'Secret' is the bond established by the abuser with the child victim. It ensures that nobody knows of the abuse other than the abuser and the abused. It is kept in place by embarrassment, fear, respect; even love."

These weapons are profoundly effective in controlling the child. They stand to be embarrassed by others discovering the secret. Clearly we live in a society that teaches us to avoid embarrassment at all costs. This is even true for young children who are taught about shame at an early age. The weapon of

20

fear speaks to the danger that the child's loved ones may face should the abuse be discovered. This includes danger the abuser may face as well, interestingly. This was what my abuser used against me...very effectively. I was responsible for his safety and I needed to protect my family. The spirit of rejection made me overly protective of anyone who was an underdog throughout my life. Respect and love of the abuser refers to the relationship that the abuser creates with the child prior to and during the process of abuse.

Often the abuser has paid attention to the child in a way that no one else has in the child's life. Needing and craving validation is a normal part of healthy development. Where the spirit of rejection is involved, normal development can become compromised. The need for validation can become extreme. This is expressed in any number of ways. We'll discuss more about it in the chapter on characteristics of a rejected personality.

To have one's sense of being and right to exist denied through sexual abuse is an ultimate form of rejection. This rejection has haunted me since then. It's made me depressed, hypervigilant, protective of children, overly responsible for others. It's taught me to have weak boundaries. I've become a care-taker whose worth is in doing, rather than in being. That I exist has never been enough for me. I had to get "it" right, though "it" was always a moving target that I could never get close enough to, to figure out what "right" was. The basic idea is that there was just something wrong with me at the core that I could never fix.

What I know for sure beyond a shadow of a doubt is that I am not alone in these experiences. According to the Darkness to Light website (www.d2l.org), a site dedicated to ending sexual abuse, in 2013, there were about 400,000 babies born in the U.S. that would fall victim to sexual abuse before

21

their 18th birthday, an overwhelmingly staggering statistic. This also speaks to the prevalence of the spirit of rejection.

What's interesting to me is that even under the influence of the rejection spirit I never wandered far from God. He has always been with me, somewhere close like sweet music playing the background. I'm not sure, though, that I ever fully trusted or believed Him for my life. I would allow Him to speak through me and heal through me, by the thousands. Just was never sure He was there for me.

I recall at age 9 going to the hospital with my mother to see my God Mother who had a tumor and was scheduled for surgery the following day. I laid hands on her and prayed and the tumor was healed. The doctors were astonished and amazed and the procedure was cancelled. There was no need for it. This was the first evidence that I had been blessed with the gift of healing. Many more such experiences were to come.

This may have been when the suicide demon was assigned to me and began to torment me. It is common for this demon to accompany the spirit of rejection. My first suicide attempt was at age 12. There was an almost constant voice that I heard speaking to me. It would tell me, "Nobody loves you," and "You'd be better off dead," or "Everybody would be better off if you weren't here. Kill yourself. Everybody would be better off if you die. Nobody loves you. Everyone would be free from you and they'd be happy. You're not worth living. Take your life. Everything would be easier for everyone if you weren't here." It was relentless and never stopped echoing in my head. And the background music of the Lord played on. I was still able to pray for the sick and see them recover. I was still speaking the Lord's Word through prophecy and seeing it come to pass. The Lord was still faithful to work through me and I was still yielded to him for His glory.

Contact Prophetess Tyson at
www.prophetessyolandadtyson.com

Around age 14, I found my mother's Tylenol pills with codeine and took as many as were in the bottle. There were quite a few, though I don't know the actual number. I recovered without going to the hospital. My family immediately enrolled me in counseling. Still I never divulged the molestation. Still I felt responsible for everyone's safety and well-being, just like he'd told me I was.

Around that same time, they told my mother that she would one day find me dead in an alley with the lifestyle I had taken on. It's true I was running with a tough crowd but the Lord was still faithful.

I recall an incident that happened while I was sitting in a crack house. I was on a sofa in front of a picture window. The Spirit of the Lord spoke to me and told me to leave immediately. I got up, told everyone goodbye and made my exit. I think I got about 3 houses away when the house was shot up exactly where I was sitting. The Lord has truly always been with me.

Even at my most scandalous, I would threaten to beat down someone unless they said the Lord's Prayer or the 23rd Psalm, completely, with no stumble, no mistakes. Generally, these were bullies who had been beating up the smart kids for no other reason than that they were smart. That infuriated me. Actually, it was part of the spirit of rejection. I became the caretaker for the vulnerable and the victimized. I thought it was absolutely unacceptable and intolerable for people to be hurt just because they were different, in this case, smart nerdy-types. I developed something of a reputation for being tough and no nonsense. I developed the keen ability to shut myself off from my feelings and to focus on doing. I'm a great do-er. Even now. Which goes right along with the spirt of rejection. I focused on doing to prove my worth. Feelings were too hard to process, too overwhelming. It was easier not to feel. Just do.

23

I was drinking by the time I turned 14, also typical of abuse survivors. Watch any episode of the television show, "Intervention," to see the pattern. Many abuse victims turn to alcohol and other substances to deaden the emotional pain of the abuse. Though around harder street drugs daily, alcohol was the only thing I would touch. No drugs, nothing harder or more destructive. I wasn't into mixing things or anything like that. The alcohol was destructive enough. I could throw back a couple of pints with no problem and still drive, still "pull it off." There were a couple of times when I don't know how I got home and the sideways angle of the parked car clearly spoke to how wasted I was. I learned that if I had Apple Now-n-Later candy and Halls lozenges that I could cover the scent of the alcohol from my mother as I raced passed her to my room when I got home.

I gave my life back to Christ at 16 and tried to kill myself for the third time. This time it was sleeping pills, a whole lot of 'em. I was completely disappointed when I woke up the next morning. You couldn't even tell that I had taken anything. There was no residue whatsoever.

At 18 I accepted the call on my life to preach and tried to blow my brains out. I put the bullet in the gun, placed the gun to my head and pulled the trigger. Nothing. I put the gun down and the bullet literally fell out of the gun and rolled across the table.

It seemed that every time God would come closer and I accepted the next level of relationship with Him, I would hear the enemy's voice louder and stronger convincing me to kill myself.

The spirit of rejection continued to plague me. It continued to harass me, blame and ridicule me, ceaselessly. It continued to tell me how worthless I was and how unloved,

24

unlovable, and burdensome I was to everyone in my life. It continued to point out how much better everyone would be if I took my life.

I tried suicide for the fifth time with my mother's hypertension medication. The doctor's said that my heart should have burst. My kidneys should have shut down. I was semi-comatose and could hear every word they said. "We don't know. She could go either way," they told my mother. They forced tar into my belly through a tube through my nose. I heard my mother praying, "You shall live and not die. You shall declare the works of the Lord." Soon after, I woke up.

I was discharged to an inpatient psychiatric facility. A woman there, soon after my arrival, told me, "There is a call on your life. God is really going to use you." I was angry that I had not been successful, again, in ending my life. Not having a whole lot of God to hold on to I made it clear to her that I didn't want to hear any of that God stuff. I just wanted to die like the voice kept telling me to.

One day, after I'd tried to hang myself in the closet at the facility, I was on 1:1. A staff person was assigned to me and only me. I had graduated from the padded cell. There I was not allowed to have clothes or anything that I could potentially hurt myself with and was monitored 24/7 by camera. It was more humiliating than I can describe. This day, as I was lying on my bed, looking out of the window, the room filled with the Presence of the Lord. The light was so bright it filled the room and shone out the window in the door into the hallway. From the midst of the Light, the Lord spoke, "Every time you desired to kill yourself, for this cause I stood in the gap. You shall preach my word in season and out of season, you shall lay hands on the sick and they shall recover. You shall declare my word, saith the Lord." And so it is. The staff came running from all over the place, seeing the Light in the room. They

25

thought maybe I'd opened the window and was trying to jump out of it. They were all touched by the glory of the Lord. And still I never divulged the molestation. It was as if I still couldn't tell anyone for fear of someone being hurt by my actions even years later. The seven year old me still took this responsibility very seriously. I would come to discover that this, too, is fairly typical of abuse survivors.

It wasn't until I was in my twenties that I began to acknowledge the abuse. Until then I didn't even know it existed. It was so far away from my consciousness that I literally did not know it had happened. God started to reveal it to me in dreams. The abuse had started around my birthday. Every birthday for years from that time was torture for me. A few days before, the nightmares of being molested would start. In my dreams I would be fighting for my life. Telling my abuser, "No!" and "Stop!" Things I could never say to him at the time. My dreams were full of experiences where I was running and fighting. Always trying to protect myself or someone else.

God is the author of this work and I am His humble vessel. What is shared here has its origin in Him. There is so much that He wants for His people, His precious children. So much He has in store for them that love Him and are the Called according to His purpose. The problem is that the spirit of rejection keeps many of us who love Him from accepting fully His grace, His mercy, His lovingkindness, His provision, His sacrifice and His finished works.

What I know for sure is that there is no way we can be who He called us to be, have what He destined us to have or do what He created us to do until we are free and delivered from the spirit of rejection. There is no way we can even begin to have the closeness with Him that He so desires. The closeness that gives our life meaning will continue to elude us until we

26

are free of the spirit of rejection. We can't even fathom the magnitude of what we're missing in our walk with Him, in our relationship with Him, until we overcome the spirit of rejection.

So what is on the other side of rejection?

What are we missing?

Here's my take on what life with God is like.

First off, He's made promises to us that only He can keep. A promise is only as good as the Promiser to keep it. The spirit of rejection will keep you from seeing fully the wonder of His promises. It keeps you from allowing Him to bless you to the extent that He wants to and can. The spirit of rejection will have you questioning God and His promises. "If He promised it, then when is He coming through with it? How long do I have to suffer? Why did I have to go through this if He's so in my corner and got all this great provision for me?" Asking these kinds of questions are the very thing that tie His hands and keep Him from being able to bless you. In that regard, you are not submitted to Him. You are believing and agreeing more strongly what the spirit of rejection is telling you. And you have whatsoever things you say, believing (Mark 11:23).

What does He tell us about His promises to us?

1. First, God promises to keep His promises that He would be glorified in them through us. How about that? He gets the glory in keeping His promises to us. 2 Corinthians 1:20 - For all the

27

promises of God in him are yea, and in him Amen, unto the glory of God by us.

2.   God promises us, by faith, victory over death through the resurrection of Jesus Christ. In I Corinthians 15:3-4, we see, "For I delivered unto you first of all that which I also received, how that Christ died for our sins according to the scriptures, and that he was buried, and that he rose again the third day according to the scriptures" Paul goes on to say in I Corinthians 15:57, "but thanks be to God, which giveth us the victory through our Lord Jesus Christ." This points clearly to our victory over death, the gift of eternal life, by belief in the resurrection of Jesus. John 10:27-28 tells us, "My sheep hear my voice, and I know them, and they follow me: 28 And I give unto them eternal life; and they shall never perish, neither shall any man pluck them out of my hand. John 3:16 - For God so loved the world, that he gave his only begotten Son, that whosoever believeth in him should not perish, but have everlasting life.

3.   He promises to supply our every need. The Bible, in Philippians 4:19 says: "But my God shall supply all your need according to his riches in glory by Christ Jesus".   God has committed Himself to us. He agrees and promises to provide us with food, clothing, shelter, safety, love, and salvation thru Jesus Christ. These truly are the basics of a life well-lived. His Word also says we who seek the Lord, "Shall not want for any good or beneficial thing" (Psalm 34:10). Repeatedly throughout His Word He promises to hear us in our need

and to meet our needs. He promises to take care of us and to keep us safe from all hurt, harm and danger with angels encamped around us. (Psalm 34:7)

4.   Our merciful, Almighty God has promised us that His grace is sufficient for anything we need. (II Corinthians 12:9).In fact, His grace, through our faith in Him, is even enough to provide for our salvation. Ephesians 2:8 tells us that by grace we are saved through faith, and that not of ourselves. Even the measure of faith that we have is a gift from God. Further, Romans 5:2 goes on to say that it is obedient faith that gives us access to the grace of God.

5.   God, our Father, in I Corinthians 10:13, promises to keep us from being overtaken by temptation. He promises to provide us a way of escape when we feel tempted. In Jude verse 24, He promises that He is able to keep us from falling and present us blameless before Himself; "Now unto Him that is able to keep you from falling, and to present you faultless before the presence of his glory with exceeding joy."

6.   God promises, in Romans 8:28, that all things work together for good to those who love and serve Him faithfully (Romans 8:28). God has promised it, and Romans 4:21 says, "And being fully persuaded that, what he had promised, he was able also to perform." Regardless of what the situation tells us, He is able and that's all that matters, or should matter.

29

7.   Mark 16:16 - God promises, anyone who believes in Jesus and is baptized for the forgiveness of sins is saved.

8.   Philippians 4:6-9 - Be careful for nothing; but in everything by prayer and supplication with thanksgiving let your requests be made known unto God.   John 15:7-8 - If ye abide in me, and my words abide in you, ye shall ask what ye will, and it shall be done unto you.

9.   Jeremiah 29:11 - For I know the thoughts that I think toward you, saith the LORD, thoughts of peace, and not of evil, to give you an expected end.

10.   2 Peter 1:4 - Whereby are given unto us exceeding great and precious promises: that by these ye might be partakers of the divine nature, having escaped the corruption that is in the world through lust.

11.   Psalms 23:1- The LORD is my shepherd; I shall not want.

12.   Ephesians 2:10 - For we are his workmanship, created in Christ Jesus unto good works, which God hath before ordained that we should walk in them.

13.   Romans 8:1-39 - There is therefore now no condemnation to them which are in Christ Jesus, who walk not after the flesh, but after the Spirit.

There are many more promises that God makes to His people that are revealed through a careful search of scripture. These are just a few of the highlights.

Contact Prophetess Tyson at
www.prophetessyolandadtyson.com

It is important to realize that the spirit of rejection keeps us from receiving these promises. It keeps us from fully accepting God's love and care for us making us believe that not only are we are not worthy of His sacrifice and never can be, but that there is no sacrifice, including His shed blood, that is enough to make up for our unworthiness. This is a blatant lie from the pit of hell whispered and perpetuated by the enemy to keep us bound and apart from the love for us that is in Christ Jesus. As long as our focus is on what's wrong with us and how people are out to get us or how we've been done wrong or will be, we can never draw nigh unto God. The enemy steals this place of rest from us. We'll never know the fullness of these promises realized because we'll never be in a place to accept and realize God's love for us. Knowing His love and choosing of us is what awaits us on the other side of deliverance from the spirit of rejection.

Contact Prophetess Tyson at
www.prophetessyolandadtyson.com

Chapter 2

WHERE DOES REJECTION COME FROM?

Rejection has many causes. Unfortunately it only takes a small window of opportunity for the spirit of rejection to set up a stronghold. What follows is not an exhaustive list of causes, though they may be some of the most common ones.

- Unwanted/unplanned/accidental pregnancies

- Child born the "wrong" gender

- The only child to survive after several miscarriages

- Born out of wedlock

- Not wanted by one parent or the other or both

- Abuse of any kind – sexual, physical, emotional, mental

32

- Parental Abandonment - real or imagined

- Neglect – physical, mental, emotional

- Being the product of a rape

- Being the invisible child as is commonly the middle child's experience

- Adoption – of any kind, including by relatives and non-relative adoption

- Perfectionistic parenting – the child can do nothing right or perceives this to be true

The roots of rejection often go all the way back to a very young age, even to a womb experience. As I described in my own life, I was rejected in the womb by both parents. And even though their regard for me changed over my lifetime, there had already been a window of opportunity opened for the spirit of rejection to enter and remain. This prenatal rejection is common, especially with unplanned/accidental pregnancies, an unwanted child, unmarried, uncommitted parents, rejection from the father, mother, or both, and rape.

It's safe to say that rejection starts most often with the family of origin. This makes sense because the spirit of rejection can be most effectively cause deeper wounds by using those closest to you. Because children rely on parents for their survival, the spirit of rejection is most effective when it uses the parental relationship.

Rejection can include abandonment, real or imagined, by one or both parents intentional or unintentional; children who have been released for adoption including adoption by

33

relatives; children with birth defects; birth order especially for the middle child who feels lost in comparison to the first and last (middle child syndrome); favoritism among children creating competition for parental affection and regard (I was my parents' favorite, remember my sister pushed me?); death of a parent; being neglected, overlooked and disregarded by a parent; domineering parents who demonstrate a lack of trust in the child; or perfectionistic parent for whom the child can never measure up to standard.

Often parents unintentionally open the door to rejection by offering conditional love. They make it clear that they approve of the child when they perform well and disapprove when they do not. They make no distinction between the child and their behavior. "I love you when you obey me," they may say. Or "I love you when you do well in school." Or,"I love you when you keep your room clean and do your chores without asking." Their profession of love and acceptance is completely performance based. This would insinuate that if they don't do well, they are not loved, which is the message the child gets loud and clear.

The Dynamics of Rejection

Anyone you need approval from can be a source of rejection for you. It has nothing to do with whether or not you have a positive relationship with them. It could be the most enriching association in your life and still be a source of rejection. What determines the matter is where or not you are looking to them for approval and acceptance of you. It is even possible to be rejected by a child. Have you ever seen a baby that would not go to someone and maybe even started crying at the notion? If you have a spirit of rejection you probably felt

34

bad for the other person. If they had a spirit of rejection, they may have made excuses for the baby and tried to act like it didn't matter. The more they talked about it the more it mattered. Otherwise it would have been quickly released.

Here's a typical example of how the spirit of rejection works:

A woman grew up with a father who was rarely at home and when he was, he was disengaged with the family. He spent most of his time in front to the television, avoiding his family. Her memory of life with her mother reflected her complete inability to meet her mother's standards. There was never a time that she could recall completing her chores where her mother didn't come behind her and re-do everything. It may have only been a small adjustment to straighten the silverware on the table or a slight, useless turn of a glass, but she would change everything. The woman grew up believing nothing she did was good enough. She would never be good enough or smart enough or accomplished enough to get her mother's approval. This belief colored other aspects of her personality making her avoid people to keep from being judged and criticized for not being good enough. She's built her career, correction, her life, around avoiding standing out and doing things wrong. In essence she's trying not to be rejected. It is actually to the point where she cannot look people in the eye as she passes them in the hallway at work and walks with her arms folded across her chest to create a boundary between her and the world. She questions every decision she makes. She lives practically paralyzed that she will make the wrong choice. Often she just waits until it's too late for a choice to be made and lets time make the decision for her. She is more willing to deal with the consequences of waiting too long than to be intentional in her life for fear of making a mistake. There is

35

still a self-protective-out for her that way. She doesn't really have to be responsible for her condition or situation. She has an excuse for not being perfect.

The spirit of rejection can also enter through public rejection. This includes rejection from peers; bullying; having unusual facial or body features that appear "different" from the rest of the world; racial, ethnic and religious prejudice; socioeconomic differences; mistreatment from authority figures (including teachers, coaches, and instructors); and abuse from authority figures, (both emotional and physical). Essentially any experience that causes a person to feel less than acceptable can create an opening for the spirit of rejection.

Bullying by peers has caused the loss by suicide of so many youth in recent years. This includes cyber-bullying over the internet. There have even been instances where youth were literally in the act of killing themselves. They succeeded, egged on by their internet audience.

Even parents have been involved with cyber bullying. Rather than stopping their own child from bullying, they've supported and encouraged it by bullying the same target themselves. There is an anonymity to the internet that has taken bullying to the next level. The root of rejection feeds on it. It has become easier to be rejected by people we don't know at a global level. The live streaming social media platforms are also susceptible to bullying right in the moment. Any opportunity for live-stream feedback is an opportunity for anonymous bullying and rejection.

36

How can you tell if it's the root of your issues and the source of your problems?

The Word says, *"He was despised and rejected and forsaken by men, a Man of sorrows and pains, acquainted with grief and sickness; and like One from Whom men hide their faces He was despised, and we did not appreciate His worth or have any esteem for Him."* ~Isaiah 53:3

To fully understand this, you have to look at the big picture of your life. The spirit of rejection will affect your perception of everything. Every experience, every decision, every relationship, every interaction, every thought, every word, every knee-jerk reaction will be influenced by the spirit of rejection. Rejection and experiences of rejection will seem to surround the person who has the spirit of rejection. It shows up everywhere, even where there really is no rejection.

The only "reality" that the person with a spirit of rejection knows is that they've been hurt by someone's words or actions towards them. They tend to be overly sensitive to being mistreated, overlooked, not wanted, not loved, not respected, not appreciated, not protected, not desired, not admired, and the list goes on. If someone didn't give a compliment the way they thought it should have been given, they've been rejected and unappreciated. If someone didn't apologize the "right" way with the "right" words, they've been rejected and disrespected. If someone didn't acknowledge them the "right" way, they've been rejected, overlooked and unappreciated. Rejection happens when a waitress has not served them well. Rejection happens when they've gone to extraordinary efforts to be accepted or special and no one

37

notices. They find rejection and disrespect everywhere, even from pets and inanimate objects.

People with a spirit of rejection may go to extremes where giving is concerned. They may give their last or they may be tight with their giving. Those who give their last on some level have issues with knowing someone else is suffering such that they put themselves in a difficult place. Somehow it seems better to them that they suffer than that someone else does.

The core fear is that they will be rejected if they don't help by giving their last, whether anyone else knows it's their last or not is irrelevant. They know and they know they've done their best. The other part of this scenario is that they take on the responsibility of other's lives. I'll get into the issues of boundaries as we proceed, suffice it to know right now that the spirit of rejection creates poor boundaries. It muddies the waters of self-not self, me-not me, mine-not mine.

On the other hand, the other extreme is that they refuse to be put out or inconvenienced. This is particularly true since they have not been appreciated sufficiently for their past giving and they have not been adequately compensated or acknowledged for their efforts. People on this end of the spectrum are just as likely to take back any gift they've given for the lack of adequate appreciation. Further there is a sense that because they have not been appreciated, they are somehow due more from everyone.

Generally they feel they will be left out of what they deserve. They feel they have been repeatedly overlooked for receiving their just due. They somehow feel, when they see others prospering or succeeding, that they have been left out and disregarded by God and everyone. They ask themselves, "Why am I not reaping as I have sown?" "Why are they

38

allowed to get over on me?" "Why are they doing so well when I've been at this so much longer?" "How can God bless them when we can see their sin and I've been trying so hard to please Him and treat people with love?"

They find themselves, very often, screaming, "It's not fair!" Yet, when they are acknowledged, it's never enough to make up for the lack of appreciation they've suffered to this point. In fact there are never enough accolades to fill the hole of rejection in their spirit. They could win an Academy Award for their performance and it would not be enough if every succeeding project didn't win one as well. And if they won one for each and every performance thereafter, they would not be satisfied until they had won the coveted EGOT – Emmy, Grammy, Oscar and Tony. Only a handful of performers in history have had such accomplishment and for the rejection spirit, their career has meant nothing until they were in that number.

For the spirit of rejection, the chase is on to be extraordinary. Depending on the person and their lives, the goal may not be to be extraordinary on a global level, unless there are other spirits influencing the pathway. The goal may be to simply be chosen and identified as outstanding in some regard. For the spirit of rejection, this is incredibly important. It is possible that entire lives are lived in an effort to be acknowledged as great, wonderful, special, unique, and extraordinary.

The irony is that they never seem to accomplish the goal. Because the spirit of rejection is still in charge, they always fall short. Something happens to take their eye off of where they are headed. One of the spirits that work in tandem with the spirit of rejection is the spirit of distraction. This causes the slightest thing to sabotage progress and thus the goal

39

of being special and over the top successful, or just special and successful at all, can be derailed. And the quest continues.

The rejection sufferer cannot see themselves inside of this life because the spirit of rejection colors their understanding to make them justified and right about their experience. The feelings of rejection become "normal" and a given way of being. It becomes the ordinary take on life rather than the influence of something not Godly.

Here's a typical example.

Imagine going to a restaurant and not being seated immediately. Others who came in behind you are seated. You begin to feel overlooked. You've been patient. It happens again. Anger starts to rise. Rather than seeking an understanding of the situation, the spirit of rejection immediately interprets that as an injustice and you leave, vowing to never return to that place again, ever. How dare they! What you didn't know is that the establishment had call-ahead seating and these patrons had been waiting in their cars already in line ahead of you. What it looked like to the spirt of rejection was that they were being given preferential treatment ahead of you.

Here's another.

Have you ever been in a conversation with someone about something really important to you and it seemed the other person was just not paying attention to what you were saying? Here you are pouring your heart out to them. And they are preoccupied with something else. How could they treat you that way if they say they love you? How could anything be more important than you in this moment? How could they not hear you when this is clearly something so important to you? They're rejecting you. You're not important. They don't love you or they would put everything aside for you…right now…because you want to/need to talk…right now…you're sharing your heart…right now…you need them to hear you…right now…you need to share this again…right now…you need to talk this out…right now…you need to scrape the bottom of this…right now…you need to feel loved…right now…you need to feel valued…right now…you need to feel heard…right now…never mind it's 3 in the morning and you woke them up from a sound sleep…never mind they said they had to go 15 minutes ago…never mind they were in the middle of something else and told you it's not a good time to talk…never mind they aren't feeling well…never mind anything about them. They're not paying attention to you right now and you feel rejected. See, the spirit of rejection will make everything be about how someone else has rejected you. It keeps you from considering your part in creating the situation, as in the timing of your request. It's impulsive and demanding. It can't wait but must be responded to immediately. It has you set up situations where you are bound to be rejected and have your feelings hurt so you can be right about how people carelessly, routinely and soundly reject you. The spirit of rejection keeps you from being responsible or accountable in anything where you feel rejected. If you are able to take some sense of responsibility, the spirt still twists the interpretation around to an, "I only did that because you did this" kind of explanation, so you're still not accountable. It's still not your fault and you're still not to blame for how you feel. Starting to get the picture?

Here's another example. We'll call them Personal Declarations. I know of someone who had a personal victory, a promotion at work. The promotion came with a significant raise and increase in responsibility and she struggled with whether or not to share it with a close family member. Although she was really excited about the accomplishment she

41

downplayed it in the sharing of it because she was already not feeling loved and appreciated.

It was a "By the way," kind of story as she told it. The reason she shared it that way, even though it was an over the top kind of experience for her, was so that if the person wasn't excited for her she was trying not feel too disappointed by the response she was anticipating from them. The spirit of rejection knows no boundaries and tries to control even the responses and reactions of others. What it fails to realize is that we reap what we sow. To expect to be disappointed is to create opportunities to be disappointed. To expect to be rejected is to create opportunities to be rejected, over and over and over again.

So what happened when she shared the accomplishment? You got it. The response matched the energy she had about it. It was a matter of fact, "oh, okay," kind of reaction. And still she was disappointed. Still she wanted them to know how important this was to her without her having to say it. They were supposed to just know. The spirit of rejection creates unreasonable expectations about how we think we should be regarded. It expects others to be mind-readers. It suggests that, "If you loved me, you'd know. I shouldn't have to say a word."

The Personal Declaration is, "I'll never share anything important with anyone again. I'll just keep it to myself like I should have anyway." Have you ever said something like, "They'll never have a chance to hurt me again. I'm done. That's the last time I put myself out there to have my feelings hurt." That is the spirit of rejection at work.

Contact Prophetess Tyson at
www.prophetessyolandadtyson.com

The Influence of Abuse on the Spirit of Rejection

Those of us who have been subjected to abuse often grow up with unresolved emotional wounds. These emotional wounds need to be treated. As it is in the natural so it is in the spiritual. Left alone, they can fester and become worse. The Enemy comes to steal, kill and destroy (John 10:10). He takes full advantage of any opening he can, including emotional wounds that are unacknowledged and untreated.

Sepsis is a blood infection that enters into the body in one place, like through an open wound, then attacks the whole system. That's what the enemy does. Once he has an entry way to the spirit that is ignored, like he does through abuse, he'll take over the whole body, mind and spirit if he can.

He wants us to only pay attention to what is wrong in our lives. He wants us to create a negative focus on life that takes over. Our self-concept, relationships, expectations and everything become negative. We may not even be aware of the negativity. Many times it is in our subconscious just below the level of the voice in our heads. It doesn't even always have words. It may only be a tightening in our shoulders or neck. It could be the headache that we cannot get rid of. It could be the insomnia that keeps us rest-broken.

The enemy especially wants us to have a negative relationship with God. Ultimately, he wants us to develop a false personality. He wants us to be ignorant of our true identity in Christ. The more we buy into his lies, the stronger he becomes an influence in our lives. The spirit of rejection feeds on identity issues and self-worth. Anything that compromises our sense of self, is a foothold for rejection. Anytime we trust someone else to tell us who we are and what our worth is we are open to the spirit of rejection. For children,

43

that is often our parents and other authority figures, including abusers.

The root of rejection keeps us from seeing who we are in Christ. The Word of God says that we are fearfully and wonderfully made (Psalm 139:14). This means that we are made by God and He is pleased with His creation. His pleasure extends to each one of us individually. Think about it. Our uniqueness is already created in us. Not one of our fingerprints is the same. Our ear prints are unique. So are our foot prints. At the cellular level our DNA is completely unique unless we are identical twins. We are unique expressions of God. Perfect in that completion even before we breathed our first breath.

When your identify it based on something other than the Truth you are susceptible to a life of great disappointment and hurt. It places the control of your feelings outside of yourself. Instead of being grounded in what God says about you, we base our identity on what others say and think. If they think we are special, then we feel special. If they disapprove of us, then we are disappointed and hurt. Unless the world thinks we are extraordinary, we feel rejected and worthless.

Anytime we place the definition of our identity outside of God it will be unstable. The song writer said "On Christ the solid rock I stand, all other ground is sinking sand," (My Hope is Built on Nothing Less). When it comes to the basis of our identity, it has to be rooted and grounded in God not in the world and people's opinion. This is critical to a life in Him. We can never even come remotely close to receiving the fullness of His finished works apart from Him. We were created for and by His good pleasure. He never intended for us to live apart from Him in any way. That is why we have been reconciled to Him through Christ. We are new creations in Him. And our identity is to be based in Him and Him alone. We become practically immune to the effects of rejection when we are

44

grounded in God. His Word says, He keeps us in perfect peace when our minds are stayed on Him (Isaiah 26:3). Unfortunately, the spirit of rejection will keep your mind stayed on rejection rather than on the Lord.

You may have seen yourself in the above examples. They may have really hit a cord. There are other ways the spirit of rejection shows up as well. Let's look now at some more specific characteristics of the rejected person

Contact Prophetess Tyson at
www.prophetessyolandadtyson.com

Chapter 3

The Rejected Personality

The spirit of rejection also shows up as a personality. It is important to know that the rejection personality has certain identifiable characteristics that are also influenced by spirits that work together with the spirit of rejection. The combination of these spirits completes the picture of the rejected person's perspective and experience. The Word of God speaks to how spirits work together in one person, like the legion of spirits that inhabited the man in Mark 5:9 (Then Jesus asked him, "What is your name? "My name is Legion," he replied, for we are many.) What is significant to know is that spirits act together specifically to accomplish or achieve an outcome. Together they manifest a personality that is distinguishable from other personality types. Where the spirit of rejection is concerned, different spirits come together to provide certain aspects and behaviors of the rejection personality. These are some of the characteristics and spirits that come with the spirit of rejection.

1. Insecurity/Inferiority.

Contact Prophetess Tyson at
www.prophetessyolandadtyson.com

This is a major issue. I put them together because they play on each other. When someone feels insecure it's largely because they feel inferior in some way. Again, the spirit of rejection causes an over-arching sense of inferiority. You just can never measure up, no matter what. Life becomes an effort to prove your worth. And it never happens. It's important to note that this is all from the experience and perspective of the spirit of rejection. There may or may not be any real cause to feel insecure and certainly no reason to feel inferior. We are all created in the image and likeness of God, joint heirs with Christ. There is no reason for anyone to feel inferior when they are rooted and grounded in their true identity in Christ.

2. Self-accusation

Closely associated with insecurity and inferiority is self-accusation. The spirit of rejection, even at a subconscious level, will make the person believe there must be something wrong with them that can never be fixed. The core belief is developed that makes them feel broken beyond repair. This belief keeps them from fully accepting the finished works of Christ because they believe not even He can heal them.

3. Fantasy

This relates to creating a whole world of make-believe. The fantasy games arena represents this characteristic. Romance novels are another aspect of fantasy. Any activity that causes the participant to create an imaginary world that they can disappear into is part of fantasy. It is ultimately creating an environment where they can never be rejected. Another aspect of fantasy is

47

lying. The rejected person creates a situation or condition where they will be accepted or avoid the disapproval of another. They lie to protect themselves from being rejected. They may then have to lie to cover for the first lie and so it goes.

4. Perfectionism

With the picture we've painted so far, it's easy to imagine how perfectionism might follow along with inferiority, insecurity and fantasy. It is an attempt to compensate for what the spirit of rejection has convinced them they lack. The spirit of rejection demands that everything be done perfectly so there is nothing that can cause them to be rejected. It even demands perfection from others that might even slightly reflect back on them. The spirit of perfectionism can show up as obsessive compulsive behaviors, legalistic religious practices, criticism and judgmental comments, having standards for others that they don't hold themselves to or being hypocritical, being short-tempered and nitpicky. No one, including themselves, can meet the demands of perfection they require. This again creates a situation where they may be rejected because they have become so difficult to live with. Interestingly, this opens a door through which other spirits enter, namely pride and vanity.

5. Pride and vanity

Pride and vanity are spirits that help to compensate for the spirit of rejection. They make the spirit of rejection feel better about itself. It redefines the unending demands of perfectionism with softer, more socially acceptable terms. No one is good enough and no one measures up to their high standards. That is not their fault. They are the ones who set the standard that everyone else should be trying to meet. Period.

6. Inequity

For the rejected personality, life is generally unfair. There is no justice, especially where they are concerned. Basically everyone has it better than they do and they may have gotten that way on the back of the rejected person. Somehow everyone has gotten over on them using their information, expertise and resources. They may spend hours on the internet obsessed with seeing how so many people are being blessed before them. Most of the people they are focused on, by their definition, are either not trying as hard as they, have not been in the game as long as they have been or are not nearly as deserving as they are to succeed. On a greater level the rejected person may take on the fight for those who they feel have been victimized by society. They take on a false sense of responsibility for those who have a cause. They fight for animal rights. They fight for homosexual rights and transgender rights. They fight for civil rights. They fight for prisoners' rights. They fight because there is a fight. It becomes a natural, safe outlet for the anger, resentment, rebellion and bitterness they already feel.

7. Hyper-Sensitivity

The spirit of rejection is super sensitive to other people's responses or reactions to them. Their feelings are on their sleeves. They are easily hurt and offended. It becomes a delicate balance for their friends and family to relate to them without hurting their feelings or offending them. Every word or action could be the one that sends them over the edge that they are already balancing on precariously. Because they are hypervigilant for where they may be rejected, they also tend to reject before they can be rejected. It is an effort to control the situation by managing the inevitable. They fully expect to be rejected and feel a sense of control by beating the other person to the punch. Then there is the issue of perceiving rejection where there really is none. An example of this may be when something doesn't happen that they expected to, like a phone call doesn't isn't made at a certain time. Or someone doesn't seek them out to speak to specifically in a room full of people. Without any other explanation even being considered, they jump right to the assumption that they've been rejected. The spirit of rejection sets it up this way because its purpose is to increase and maintain our experience of being rejected.

8. Martyrdom

The rejected person often goes to a place of martyrdom when they've been confronted about their behavior. They may not invite anyone else to their pity party but the "woe is me" is flows abundantly. They become the worst person in the world with no way to be forgiven. Not even the Blood of Jesus is enough to cover their iniquities and the wrongness of their being. They're sorry and they'll never bother you again as long as they live. They'll never need anything from anyone for the rest of their lives and yours. They decide to suffer in silence. No punishment is enough or too great. If they lost their all, were put in solitary confinement for life and had their tongues cut out so as to never utter

50

another offending word, it wouldn't match their wrongness. From this space, it is impossible for them to fully receive the gift of salvation and forgiveness.

9. Lust

You may be saying at this point that this one doesn't have anything to do with you. After all, you don't sleep around, you don't have a lot of sexual partners. Hear me out on this because that is not the only way this spirit shows up. This characteristic has to do with finding substitutes for real love. From a sexual perspective, this includes homosexuality and lesbianism, masturbation, incest, sexual relations outside of marriage, seduction, and incest. From a non-sexual understanding, it can include materialism, gluttony, food addiction and over-eating, alcohol and drug addictions, and other strange and unusual addictions, including addictions to shopping, social media, sniffing gasoline and other substances, overindulging in any one particular food like ketchup, tartar sauce, BBQ sauce, sugar, potato chips and other carbohydrates. These are all substitutes for feeling loved. The rush from these indulgences causes the same release of dopamine that mimics the feeling of being in love.

10. Apathy

The spirit of apathy is often associated with the spirit of rejection. For the rejected person it becomes harder and harder to muster the energy to live life. They have lived so engaged and involved with controlling and pleasing everyone else that they have no energy for their own lives. Burnout ensues and any effort becomes too much.

51

To get up in the morning is a chore. What follows is the challenge to care about anything related to anything. The primary desire becomes to want to run away from everything. Not to start over. Even a fresh start takes too much energy, though it is enticing to dream about. They just want to stop life the way it is and not have to do anything. Nothing is important anymore. Apathy causes lethargy, depression, sadness, despair, discouragement, despondency, grief, hopelessness, insomnia, negativity, and so much more that feels overwhelming and inescapable. It's immobilizing. It leaves the person just wanting to be taken care of.

11. Indecisiveness

Another spirit that causes the rejected person to be immobilized is the spirit of indecisiveness. The Word of God says that a double minded man is unstable in all of his ways (James 1:8). Indecision can result in making no decision, changing one's mind repeatedly. The spirit of fear may also be involved in being afraid to make a decision. This fear may lead back to being apathetic, too immobilized to care and too burnout to do anything.

12. Depression

Depression is sort of the background music for the spirit of rejection. It is always somewhere lurking close by. Anything that we've already mentioned could be the tipping point into depression. It's part of the double-mindedness. According to the World Health Organization Depression Fact Sheet (www.who.int/mediacentre/factsheets/fs369/en/), there are about 350 million people worldwide who suffer with depression. Often associated with the spirit of

52

death, there are 800,000 people who succumb to suicide from depression each year and it is the second leading cause of death in 15-28 year olds.

13. Shame

Shame is the sense that something is intrinsically wrong with you. It is self-condemnation and unworthiness. On no level is the rejected person able to see anything of value in themselves whether consciously or subconsciously, which is where it primarily lives. Like depression, shame plays always in the background for the rejected person. It is the stage on which their life is played. It colors everything giving the rejected person the lens of interpretation. The rejected person through shame can never be enough. They can never measure up to be acceptable and approved of in life.

14. Fear

The spirit of fear is pervasive. The Word even mentions it in direct opposition to the Holy Spirit: Perfect love casts out all fear (1 John 4:18). There is no end to the things that the rejected person may be afraid of. It covers everything from water, dirt, abandonment, failure, rejection, dying alone, marriage, dogs, cats, germs, the dark, driving, expressway driving, ladders, commitment, accidents, confrontation, you name it and someone is afraid of it. The spirit of rejection also fears standing out and being noticed and being judged, criticized and found lacking. It seems safer to blend in and stay under the radar. Rejection also fears being wrong or stupid, making a mistake or being a fraud. An extreme of this spirit is panic attacks and the like.

Contact Prophetess Tyson at
www.prophetessyolandadtyson.com

Anxiety, worry and nervousness is another demonic aspect of the spirit of fear.

15. Suspiciousness

The spirit of rejection has the tendency to be suspicious of everyone that has the potential to reject them. It makes up reasons and expectations to explain their suspicions. The story may be completely based on their own projections and interpretations of "evidence." Nothing can convince them that it isn't true. It's true simply because they think it. Even dreams are believed and can increase the suspiciousness. It is actually a defense mechanism to keep them from being rejected by keeping others away with their suspicions of their ill-meaning intentions. This spirit of suspiciousness is especially prevalent when the spirit of grandiosity is also present. This has the rejected person obsessed with extravagance, power and fame. It also has the rejected person obsessed with losing it. The result is accusing and blaming others for their failure or for holding them back. They make decisions based on fear of someone denying them their opportunity for greatness. All of this being rooted and grounded in the subjective interpretation of someone else's motives and intentions. The spirit of rejection never rests from believing others have negative intentions towards them and continues to watch carefully for subjective "evidence" that confirms their suspicions.

16. Blame

Because the spirit of rejection so fears being rejected, it has difficulty accepting responsibility for anything that could be perceived as failure or negative. It often refers

54

back to the reason for its behavior or choices as being a response to what someone else did. "I only did that because you did that." Everyone and everything is blamed for their circumstances not being what they want them to be. These feelings may swing right over into martyrdom and self-condemnation. Part of this tendency to blame includes blaming God. It's a faith challenge. Rather than being accountable for decisions and choices, it is easier from the perspective of rejection to just blame Him for not coming through. It's easier to blame Him for not blessing them the way He could and promised He would. Blaming God may also include a sense that He is always angry and disappointed in them. And what chance do they have if God Himself is against them? It is this kind of faulty reasoning the keeps the person with a spirit of rejection bound.

17. Love Starved

The spirit of rejection results in the person feeling completely starved for love and genuine regard. Nothing is ever enough from their family or significant other to make them feel loved and validated. There isn't enough time spent with them. There aren't enough gifts given. There's never enough consideration. This is fed by the hypervigilant watch for rejection and validated when they find reason to believe it.

No one with a spirit of rejection will have all of these characteristics. You can see, however, that often they are interrelated and play on each other intimately. At different times one may be more prevalent than another. They may also develop over time as the experiences of life unfold. They may also intensify over time as there are more experiences of

55

rejection. To that extent the spirt of rejection confirms itself by continuing to interpret rejection in more and more areas and aspects of life. The rejection story becomes a self-fulfilling prophecy.

Too often when we feel rejected it is through a faulty interpretation of events. We immediately feel hurt when we don't get the reaction we wanted and make it mean something is wrong with us. I can recall many times feeling overlooked in the ministry, feeling that I had not received the honor I deserved, that I was not being treated the way I should have. What was wrong with me? Why don't they like me? Why do they treat me this way? It seemed everyone around me was being blessed and still I was overlooked. Why didn't God bless ME? It seemed like I could look at so many people around me that were not trying as hard as I was to please the Lord and still I struggled with depression and finances and feeling loved. There seemed to be nowhere I could turn to make sense of my life outside of the perception and interpretation of the spirit of rejection. I had no other explanation than that there was something wrong with me.

The spirit of rejection will have you comparing yourself endlessly with other people and their situations. You always come out the loser, no matter what. There is nothing that you can do to make a difference. Nothing is ever enough to make you compare. No matter how long you've been at the game, they are getting the results you want that somehow continue to evade you. Your song is, "What Have I Done So Wrong?"

The spirit of rejection makes you feel like life has passed you by. You've wasted your youth and your vitality and you can never get it back. No matter how old or how young you are, it's too late to do anything worthwhile and meaningful now. You've missed your chance. I spent a lot of time lamenting how I never finished college. I always felt like my

56

life was just a waste. My believing that made it easier for the enemy to convince me to kill myself. What would the loss be exactly? From all I could tell, not much. Because your self-worth is based on the spirit of rejection, there is nothing anyone can say or do that makes you believe you are deserving or worthwhile. Not even God Himself could convince me that I was worthwhile and wouldn't be better off dead.

You may be drawn to situations where you stand out for your accomplishments. In the church world, it may be that you have a greater donation, tithe or giving than others. You take some satisfaction in that you are being seen standing in the "$1000 line." The opposite is also true. You experience a great level of shame in not being in the special line. Or you may have nothing at all to give. In fact, before you go, you may make the decision to stay home if you can't stand out. Another aspect of this is having to prove yourself publically. You must be conceived of as the smartest, most accomplished, most in the know, most aware, most everything. This is the only way to prove that you deserve to exist and should not be rejected. Again, your worth is based on your doing, rather than your being.

You set up situations to be recognized by leadership. It's important because it means you're chosen and special. When that doesn't happen, your feelings are hurt and you feel unloved and overlooked. Your response may be two-fold. You're angry at being overlooked and you're hurt by not being acknowledged. You make up a story about why it didn't happen that leaves you justified in your feelings. You make a Personal Declaration to never return to that situation to be ignored again. Additionally, you are easily offended if leadership corrects or disciplines you. This can be privately or publically. Even if you are the only one who knows, the embarrassment you feel can be so overwhelming it almost physically hurts. You are devastated that anyone pointed out

57

anything that you could improve. Even if there are things to improve, the shame in someone noticing that is the issue.

You are convinced that you could do a better job than any leader in any leadership position. Your ideas are better. Your approach is more prosperous and appropriate. You have what it takes to move the situation forward. Period. All you need is the opportunity to prove you're right.

The spirit of rejection will have you convinced you have the answers to everyone else's life. In their best interest you willingly share your insight and plans to make their lives better while yours may be secretly in shambles. This attempt to fix everyone is actually an effort to play God. You assume because, of course, you're right about everything, that you have the authority to step in. Your identity is wrapped up in having other peoples' answers. You are in your world when people seek you out for your advice. You may become angry or frustrated when your advice is not used. You may feel taken for granted and taken advantage of. You may make a Personal Declaration to not help again since you were so unappreciated.

The spirit of rejection makes you feel like an outsider. You are super sensitive to being left out of relationships and conversations. You never feel chosen. You never feel included. You feel like everyone has secrets or has information they are not sharing with you. The spirit of rejection has you set up situations of you-versus-them, "them" being the rest of the world. Rarely do you have a sense of team or support, even if support is there. The spirit of rejection will keep you feeling like you are all alone on your own forever and ever and ever. By focusing on how much support you don't feel you have you miss the support you have. By only seeing how you've been left out you miss how much inclusion there is.

Contact Prophetess Tyson at
www.prophetessyolandadtyson.com

Being left out is the ultimate representation of rejection. For the spirit of rejection, there are almost no bounds to what it will do to be included. It will have you constructing experiences and "truths" about yourself in order to be accepted. Nothing so outlandish that it could never be but not the truth either. The need is to fit in and to be validated by someone whose approval you need. In some instances, the spirt of rejection will have you create something of an alter ego. This is a complete false self. One that you feel is acceptable to others where you are not.

There are other characteristics of rejection that have not been covered in detail here. Qualities like envy, jealousy, hatred, criticism, judgement and stubbornness are all associated with the spirit of rejection. In all honesty, any negative emotional experience could possibly be rooted in rejection. As I mentioned, not everyone will have every characteristic discussed here. It is possible that some may be more prevalent than others and they may become worse over time. The unchecked spirit of rejection and its demonic companions grow in power and influence as life rolls on.

59

Chapter 4

What Does the Bible Say About Rejection and Your True Identity?

Psalm 27:10 (KJV)

10 When my father and my mother forsake me, then the Lord will take me up.

2 Corinthians 12:9 (KJV)

9 And he said unto me, My grace is sufficient for thee: for my strength is made perfect in weakness. Most gladly therefore will I rather glory in my infirmities, that the power of Christ may rest upon me.

The spirit of rejection is a spirit of the anti-Christ. It stands in exact opposition to the Spirit of God. It rejects God. Think about it. Notice how the spirit of rejection focuses us on everything wrong with us. It keeps us from accepting God's love. It keeps us bound in fear of man and fear of God. When you get down to the basics of it, it is the same spirit of the enemy who was rejected from heaven. *(Ezekiel 28:17 – "Your heart became proud on account of your beauty, and you corrupted your wisdom because of your splendor. So I threw you to the earth.")* No wonder it is so prevalent in man. We were never supposed to suffer under the spirit of rejection simply based on who we are created to be in God. It is the enemy's plan to keep us as far away from the knowledge of God as he can. How better to do that than to make us believe that at our core we will never be accepted and approved of by Him or anyone else.

When we believe according to the spirit of rejection, we are essentially rejecting God's truth about us. God created us as a unique expression of His purpose, wonderfully made (Psalm 139:14). When He did that, He also made us acceptable to Him through Christ. This is the intention of redemption through the Savior's Blood: "Even before he made the world, God loved us and chose us in Christ to be holy and without fault in his eyes" (Ephesians 1:4 NLT).

Nothing we could ever do on our own could make us acceptable to and worthy of God's unending love. There is no "doing" that can accomplish that. God accepts us not from anything we did but through what Christ did for us. Christ sacrificed His life for us on the cross to cover all that is wrong (our sin) in the sight of God. So when God looks at us He sees the Blood of Jesus and says, "I accept you as you have accepted Christ. What He did for you is acceptable and now, because of Him, you are acceptable as well." All there is for us to do is to accept and submit to Christ as our Savior and our sin and wrongness is covered by His Blood.

"For not he that commendeth himself is approved, but whom the Lord commendeth. (2 Corinthians 10:18 KJV)

61

Saul, An Example of the Spirit of Rejection

Saul is a prime example of the effects of rejection. In his anger and hurt feelings, he allowed envy, jealousy, and hate to take lay hold to him. This situation is related to us in 1 Samuel 18:7-11 (KJV).

⁷ And the women answered one another as they played, and said, Saul hath slain his thousands, and David his ten thousands.

⁸ And Saul was very wroth, and the saying displeased him; and he said, They have ascribed unto David ten thousands, and to me they have ascribed but thousands: and what can he have more but the kingdom?

⁹ And Saul eyed David from that day and forward.

¹⁰ And it came to pass on the morrow, that the evil spirit from God came upon Saul, and he prophesied in the midst of the house: and David played with his hand, as at other times: and there was a javelin in Saul's hand.

¹¹ And Saul cast the javelin; for he said, I will smite David even to the wall with it. And David avoided out of his presence twice.

In this passage of scripture we see Saul being overtaken by the spirit of jealousy. It starts with the women praising David for slaying ten thousands. The women also praise Saul for slaying thousands. Clearly this is a lesser number than David. Feeling rejected for not slaying as many as David, Saul became angry at David and jealous of him and the praise he

62

received. He felt embarrassed and publically shamed. The next day, Saul became exceedingly angry. His anger was increased by the evil spirit (of jealousy) that came upon him. It became so overwhelming for him that he planned to murder David. Notice, it was not the rejection that left Saul open to the influence of the evil spirit. It was how he reacted to being rejected. It really is our reaction that dictates our outcome.

The rejection itself is not a sin. It is simply something that happens to us in the process of living. The spirit of rejection enters when we are submitted to it in our response to being rejected. Our reaction can open us up to the spirit of rejection and the spirits that accompany it. Saul became subject to rebellion, which the Bible says is as witchcraft and idol worship. This is what left him open to the attack of the evil spirit. Verse 29 says, "29 And Saul was yet the more afraid of David; and Saul became David's enemy continually." This is the result of rejection that festers and allows other spirits to become attached. 1 Samuel 15:23 (KJV) says more about Saul's demise,

> 23 For rebellion is as the sin of witchcraft, and stubbornness is as iniquity and idolatry. Because thou hast rejected the word of the Lord, he hath also rejected thee from being king.

Saul clearly lost His blessing through his weakness to the spirit of rejection.

Your True Identity: Who We are in Christ

To fully grasp this concept is to gain a strong foothold in your walk with Christ. So many believers fail to understand and apply this very simple idea yet it holds the key to living a victorious life and walking in the blessings of God. This is a

63

vital Truth of God that will truly make you free! John 8:32, tells us "And ye shall know the truth, and the truth shall make you free." Prepare to receive this truth by praying this simple prayer before you go any further:

> *"Lord, I give you all praise, all honor and all glory. I thank You that the gates of my eyes, my ears, my heart, and my understanding are open to receive Your Word of Truth concerning me. Thank you for helping me see who I am to You. Thank you for helping me to accept Your Truth as my own. I praise you that I am free from the bondage of rejection in all its forms. In the name of Jesus, I believe it is so. Amen."*

To stop believing the lies the enemy has told you through the spirit of rejection, you must begin by knowing God's Truth about you. You must begin with knowing how He regards you. The enemy has had you in bondage unnecessarily through feeding you false beliefs and false confirmation of those beliefs. He has kept you from living a life of real, grounded success. He has kept you powerless.

You may have even accepted Christ as your Savior years ago and continued to live life through the lens of rejection, lied to and deceived by the enemy. Now we know that the Blood of Jesus alone is enough to make us worthy in the sight of God. Anything that says otherwise is from the enemy. You are denying the work of the cross if you continue to speak, live and affirm your unworthiness. You are saying that Christ died for nothing. What a slap in the face of God! You have to start saying to yourself, "Jesus made me worthy! I am worthy by the Blood of the Lamb! Thank you, Jesus!"

64

The Truth about You

Here is the Truth God wants you to know and believe from here out. Once you know the Truth, you are accountable for it and can no longer walk in ignorance of it. God will help you embrace it. He wants you to know it and live it powerfully so that He can get the glory from it.

Truth #1

God loves you

God already knows every little thing about us and He still loves us, regardless. And He loved us even at our ugliest and darkest in the midst of our wrongness. The Word of God says that He loved us so much that He gave His only begotten Son, that whosoever believeth in him should not perish, but have everlasting life (John 3:16). It is important to notice here that He loved us first. He gave us the Savior even before He adopted us as His children. It is critical to notice that when He could have rejected us in our sin and wretchedness, He didn't. Instead He sent a Savior so that we would not perish. Instead He sent a Savior so that we could be found acceptable and worthy in His eyes. He sent a Savior so that He in His perfection could come closer to us and be with us. He made a way to be with us because He loves us and wants a relationship with us. Romans 5:8, "But God commendeth his love toward us, in that, while we were yet sinners, Christ died for us."

A deeper Truth may be a bit more challenging to accept though it definitely bears mentioning. God loves us with the same love that He has for Christ! He adopted us to the same

65

Contact Prophetess Tyson at
www.prophetessyolandadtyson.com

level of son-ship that Christ has in Him. The proof is in scripture. John 17:23 says, "I in them, and thou in me, that they may be made perfect in one; and that the world may know that thou hast sent me, and hast loved them, as thou hast loved me."

To go a step further, we know that Christ loved us so much that He gave His life for us. This is how much He loves us, "Greater love hath no man than this, that a man lay down his life for his friends. Ye are my friends, if ye do whatsoever I command you (John 15:13)." The spirit of rejection seeks to keep us from this knowledge. It seeks to keep us from knowing the fullness of God's love for us. Our worthiness is intimately connected to knowing how much God loves us and wants us to be blessed.

> *Ephesians 3:17-19, "That Christ may dwell in your hearts by faith; that ye, being rooted and grounded in love, May be able to comprehend with all saints what is the breadth, and length, and depth, and height; And to know the love of Christ, which passeth knowledge, that ye might be filled with all the fullness of God."*

Truth #2

You have been created to fulfill a special purpose in God's kingdom.

The Bible says in Ephesians 2:10, "For we are his workmanship, created in Christ Jesus unto good works, which God hath before ordained that we should walk in them." This speaks with clarity that we are created to do good works ordained by God. This also implies that we are created for His pleasure and to please Him with our lives. If we are living under the spirit of rejection, we can never fulfill that call. Jeremiah 29:11 says, "For I know the thoughts that I think toward you, saith the LORD, thoughts of peace, and not of evil, to give you an expected end." An expected end in God can only be for our good.

Truth #3

You are made whole, justified and declared innocent in Christ.

Once you have repented of your sins and accepted Christ as your Savior, you are forgiven of all your sin. You are justified, made acceptable, before God.

> *Galatians 2:16, "Knowing that a man is not justified by the works of the law, but by the faith of Jesus Christ, even we have believed in Jesus Christ, that we might be justified by the faith of Christ, and not by the works of the law: for by the works of the law shall no flesh be justified."*

This passage from Galatians speaks to the innocence of the believer who is justified in Christ. The word "justified" comes from the Greek word "dikaioo". It means to regard as innocent; to free or to be righteous. When a person is justified, they have been made innocent all over again. It is as if the sin never existed. It's wiped clean and they are made as white as snow.

67

Because we have been cleansed from sin by the Blood of Jesus, we deserve to have a clean, clear conscious. We have no need to feel guilty or ashamed of ourselves from a spirit of rejection. We release the need to return to our past transgressions and mistakes. According to the Word, when we accepted Christ, we became new creatures in Him, old things have passed away (2 Cor.5:17).

Truth #4

You are a new creature in Christ

Yes, you are re-born. You are brand new in Christ. 2 Corinthians 5:17, says, "Therefore if any man be in Christ, he is a new creature: old things are passed away; behold, all things are become new." This Truth is hard for many believers to grasp as well. We are re-created in righteousness and true holiness.

> *Ephesians 4:24, "And that ye put on the new man, which after God is created in righteousness and true holiness."*

And the most incredible part is that we are re-created as sons and daughters of God.

> *John 1:12-13, "But as many as received him, to them gave he power to become the sons of God, even to them that believe on his name: Which were born, not of blood, nor of the will of the flesh, nor of the will of man, but of God."*

68

Truth #5

Your sins have been forgotten

Not only have your sins been forgiven they have actually been forgotten. Because He loves us so much, He allows us to stand blameless before Him.

Hebrews 10:17, "And their sins and iniquities will I remember no more."

With our sins forgiven and forgotten, we have peace with God. We are in right standing with Him through being justified by the Blood of Christ.

Romans 5:1, "Therefore being justified by faith, we have peace with God through our Lord Jesus Christ."

Truth #6

You have authority through Christ and are seated with Him

The phrase, "To be seated" means to be in a place of authority. According to the Word of God, Jesus is seated at the right hand of God and we are seated with Christ.

Ephesians 2:6, "And hath raised us up together, and made us sit together in heavenly places in Christ Jesus."

69

This authority gives us power over all the power of the enemy (Luke 10:19). This includes power over infirmity, diseases, sickness, demons, situations and territories, etc.

Here is a list of scriptures that speak directly to your identity in Christ. Ask Him to reveal the fullness of who you are in these scriptures. Hide the Word in your heart that you would not sin against Him (Psalm 119:11).

In Him who is the Head of all things I am made whole (Colossians 2:10).

By Christ I am alive (Ephesians 2:5).

I am free from the law of sin and death (Romans 8:2).

I am established in righteousness. I am far from oppression and fear does not come near me (Isaiah 54:14).

Satan cannot touch me for I am born of God (1 John 5:18).

God has chosen me and before Him I am holy and without blame in love (Ephesians 1:4; 1 Peter 1:16).

I have the mind of Christ (1 Corinthians 2:16; Philippians 2:5).

The peace of God that passes all understanding keeps my heart and mind through Jesus Christ (Philippians 4:7).

Greater is He that is in me than he that is in the world (1 John 4:4).

Contact Prophetess Tyson at
www.prophetessyolandadtyson.com

I have the gift of righteousness and reign in life by Jesus Christ (Romans 5:17).

Putting off the old man I have put on the new man, which is renewed in the knowledge after the image of Him Who created me (Colossians 3:9-10).

I give, and it is given to me; good measure, pressed down, shaken together, and running over do men give into my bosom (Luke 6:38).

All of my needs are met for my God supplies all my needs according to His riches in glory by Christ Jesus (Philippians 4:19).

With the shield of faith, I quench all the fiery darts of the wicked (Ephesians 6:16).

I can do all things through Christ which strengthens me (Philippians 4:13).

I am of a chosen generation, a royal priesthood. God has called me out of darkness into His marvelous light and I show forth His praise (1 Peter 2:9).

I am born again of the incorruptible seed of the Word of God, which lives and abides forever (1 Peter 1:23).

I am His workmanship created in Christ Jesus unto good works (Ephesians 2:10).

I am a new creature in Christ (2 Corinthians 5:17).

I am dead to sin and alive to God by His spirit (Romans 6:11;1 Thessalonians 5:23).

I am a doer of the Word (James 1:22,25).

I am a joint-heir with Christ (Romans 8:17).

71

I am more than a conqueror through Him Who loves me (Romans 8:37).

I overcome by the blood of the Lamb and the word of my testimony (Revelation 12:11).

I am a partaker of His divine nature (2 Peter 1:3-4).

I am an ambassador for Christ (2 Corinthians 5:20).

I am the righteousness of God in Jesus Christ (2 Corinthians 5:21).

My body is the temple of the Holy Ghost; I am not my own (1 Corinthians 6:19).

I am the head and not the tail; I am above and not beneath (Deuteronomy 28:13).

I am the light of the world (Matthew 5:14).

I am redeemed through His Blood (Ephesians 1:7).

He has delivered me from the power of darkness and translated me into the kingdom of his dear son (Colossians 1:13).

I make the voice of His praise be heard (Psalm 66:8; 2 Timothy 1:9).

I am healed by the stripes of Jesus Christ (Isaiah 53:5; 1 Peter 2:24).

I am seated with Christ in heavenly places (Ephesians 2:6; Colossians 2:12).

He strengthens me with all might according to His glorious power (Colossians 1:11).

Contact Prophetess Tyson at
www.prophetessyolandadtyson.com

I resist devil in the Name of Jesus and he flees from me (James 4:7).

I press toward the mark of the prize of the high calling of God in Christ Jesus (Philippians 3:14).

God has not given me the spirit of fear; but of power, of love, and of a sound mind (2 Timothy 1:7).

Christ lives in me (Galatians 2:20).

Here are more scriptures that speak to how God relates to rejection. The Word is full of them. These are just to get you started on your healing journey.

Study:

1 Peter 2:4 (KJV)

⁴ To whom coming, as unto a living stone, disallowed indeed of men, but chosen of God, and precious,

1 Peter 5:7 (KJV)

⁷ Casting all your care upon him; for he careth for you.

Psalm 139:13-14 (KJV)

¹³ For thou hast possessed my reins: thou hast covered me in my mother's womb.

Contact Prophetess Tyson at
www.prophetessyolandadtyson.com

^{14} I will praise thee; for I am fearfully and wonderfully made: marvellous are thy works; and that my soul knoweth right well.

John 1:11 (KJV)

^{11} He came unto his own, and his own received him not.

Romans 8:31 (KJV)

^{31} What shall we then say to these things? If God be for us, who can be against us?

Philippians 4:19 (KJV)

^{19} But my God shall supply all your need according to his riches in glory by Christ Jesus.

1 Peter 5:8 (KJV)

^{8} Be sober, be vigilant; because your adversary the devil, as a roaring lion, walketh about, seeking whom he may devour:

Isaiah 49:15 (KJV)

^{15} Can a woman forget her sucking child, that she should not have compassion on the son of her womb? yea, they may forget, yet will I not forget thee.

Psalm 66:16-20 (KJV)

^{16} Come and hear, all ye that fear God, and I will declare what he hath done for my soul. ^{17} I cried unto him with my mouth, and he was extolled with my tongue. ^{18} If I regard iniquity in my heart, the Lord will

Contact Prophetess Tyson at
www.prophetessyolandadtyson.com

not hear me: [19] But verily God hath heard me; he hath attended to the voice of my prayer. [20] Blessed be God, which hath not turned away my prayer, nor his mercy from me.

Deuteronomy 14:2 (KJV)

[2] For thou art an holy people unto the Lord thy God, and the Lordhath chosen thee to be a peculiar people unto himself, above all the nations that are upon the earth.

1 Corinthians 3:16 (KJV)

[16] Know ye not that ye are the temple of God, and that the Spirit of God dwelleth in you?

Isaiah 49:16 (KJV)

[16] Behold, I have graven thee upon the palms of my hands; thy walls are continually before me.

Romans 15:13 (KJV)

[13] Now the God of hope fill you with all joy and peace in believing, that ye may abound in hope, through the power of the Holy Ghost

Jeremiah 30:17 (KJV)

[17] For I will restore health unto thee, and I will heal thee of thy wounds, saith the Lord; because they called thee an Outcast, saying, This is Zion, whom no man seeketh after.

Proverbs 16:3 (KJV)

Contact Prophetess Tyson at
www.prophetessyolandadtyson.com

³ Commit thy works unto the Lord, and thy thoughts shall be established.

Psalm 37:4 (KJV)

⁴ Delight thyself also in the Lord: and he shall give thee the desires of thine heart.

Lamentations 3:31-33King James Version (KJV)

³¹ For the Lord will not cast off for ever: ³² But though he cause grief, yet will he have compassion according to the multitude of his mercies. ³³ For he doth not afflict willingly nor grieve the children of men.

Leviticus 26:11 (KJV)

¹¹ And I set my tabernacle among you: and my soul shall not abhor you.

Colossians 1:17 (KJV)

¹⁷ And he is before all things, and by him all things consist.

Psalm 34 (KJV)

34 I will bless the Lord at all times: his praise shall continually be in my mouth. ² My soul shall make her boast in the Lord: the humble shall hear thereof, and be glad. ³ O magnify the Lord with me, and let us exalt his name together. ⁴ I sought the Lord, and he heard me, and delivered me from all my fears. [5] They looked unto him, and were lightened: and their faces were not ashamed. [6] This poor man cried, and the Lord heard him, and saved him out of all his troubles. [7] The angel of the Lord encampeth round about them that fear him, and delivereth them. [8] O taste and see that the Lord is good: blessed is the man that trusteth in him. [9] O fear the Lord, ye his saints: for there is no want to them that fear him. [10] The young lions do lack, and suffer hunger: but they that seek the Lord shall not want any good thing. [11] Come, ye children, hearken unto me: I will teach you the fear of the Lord. [12] What man is he that desireth life, and loveth many days, that he may see good? [13] Keep thy tongue from evil, and thy lips from speaking guile. [14] Depart from evil, and do good; seek peace, and pursue it. [15] The eyes of the Lord are upon the righteous, and his ears are open unto their cry. [16] The face of the Lord is against them that do evil, to cut off the remembrance of them from the earth. [17] The righteous cry, and the Lordheareth, and delivereth them out of all their troubles. [18] The Lord is nigh unto them that are of a broken heart; and saveth such as be of a contrite spirit. [19] Many are the afflictions of the righteous: but the Lord delivereth him out of them all. [20] He keepeth all his bones: not one of them is broken. [21] Evil shall slay the wicked: and they that hate the righteous shall be desolate. [22] The Lord redeemeth the soul of his servants: and none of them that trust in him shall be desolate.

Luke 6:22-23 (KJV)

[22] Blessed are ye, when men shall hate you, and when they shall separate you from their company, and shall reproach you, and cast out your name as evil, for the Son of man's sake. [23] Rejoice ye in that day, and leap

for joy: for, behold, your reward is great in heaven: for in the like manner did their fathers unto the prophets.

Romans 15:7King James Version (KJV)

[7] Wherefore receive ye one another, as Christ also received us to the glory of God.

Isaiah 52:13King James Version (KJV)

[13] Behold, my servant shall deal prudently, he shall be exalted and extolled, and be very high.

Chapter 5

How to Overcome the Spirit of Rejection

While the ideal is to have a veteran, seasoned minister take you through deliverance from the spirit of rejection, it is possible and very effective to take yourself through. You simply must follow these directions to the letter. Each step is significant and vital to your success.

It is also important to remember that even if you are completing this deliverance process on your own, you are never alone. Jesus Christ is also with you as you go through deliverance and healing from the spirit of rejection.

Here are your deliverance instructions. Follow the steps exactly as outlined.

Step 1: The Prayer of Repentance

Repentance allows us to return to right standing with God. When we confess and repent of our sins, He forgives them, casts them as far away from our presence as the east is from the west and we are made clean before Him. He alone can forgive sin and He is with you through this entire process.

Mark 2:7King James Version (KJV)

[7] Why doth this man thus speak blasphemies? who can forgive sins but God only?

Mark 1:4 King James Version (KJV)

4 John did baptize in the wilderness, and preach the baptism of repentance for the remission of sins.

Hebrews 6:6 King James Version (KJV)

6 If they shall fall away, to renew them again unto repentance; seeing they crucify to themselves the Son of God afresh, and put him to an open shame.

Psalm 103:12 King James Version (KJV)

[12] As far as the east is from the west, so far hath he removed our transgressions from us.

Contact Prophetess Tyson at
www.prophetessyolandadtyson.com

PRAY THIS OUT LOUD

- Father God, I sincerely and honestly repent of every sin that I have committed in my entire lifetime from birth to this very moment. I take full responsibility for every sin in my life. I turn away from them and promise to make a sincere effort to never commit these sins again.
- Lord Jesus, I sincerely and honestly repent of every sin I have committed in thought and imagination, word and deed that did not bring You glory.
- Father, I sincerely and honestly repent of sins of commission and sins of omission. I repent of sins known and unknown. I repent of sins intentional and unintentional. And I repent of the sins of my ancestral lineage and previous generations.
- I take full and total responsibility for my sins and wrongdoings. I ask Your forgiveness and cover every sin concerning me with the Blood of Jesus. I ask that you accept my sincere repentance of sin. (If you have sincerely, humbly and earnestly repented of your sin, then know that He has accepted it. If you have any doubt, ask Him to show you what you have not surrendered or what is blocking you. Be quiet now and listen for what the Spirit of the Lord wants you to know. When you know that God has accepted your repentance, move to step six.)
- Father I thank You for the gracious, merciful gift of forgiveness. Thank You for allowing me to be in right standing with You. I give You

81

praise, honor and glory, in the Name of Jesus. Amen.

-

Step 2: The Prayer of Salvation

The Prayer of Salvation is based on Romans 10:9-10 & Acts 2:38.

Romans 10:9-10 (KJV)

> *⁹ That if thou shalt confess with thy mouth the Lord Jesus, and shalt believe in thine heart that God hath raised him from the dead, thou shalt be saved.*
> *¹⁰ For with the heart man believeth unto righteousness; and with the mouth confession is made unto salvation.*

Acts 2:38 (KJV)

> *³⁸ Then Peter said unto them, Repent, and be baptized every one of you in the name of Jesus Christ for the remission of sins, and ye shall receive the gift of the Holy Ghost.*

According to this passage of scripture, to be saved, you must say out loud that you believe Christ died and that God raised Him from the dead. Also be willing to receive the gift of God's spirit which is the infilling of the Holy Spirit.

Contact Prophetess Tyson at
www.prophetessyolandadtyson.com

PRAY THIS OUT LOUD

- Lord Jesus....I confess before You that I have sinned and done things that are wrong in Your sight. I am truly sorry for my sins...intentional and unintentional, known and unknown, by commission and omission. I ask Your forgiveness. Please forgive me for this in particular, as it is heavy on my heart: _____. (Include specifically here whatever you feel especially troubled about.
- I believe in my heart that You, Lord Jesus, in Your innocence chose to die for me to take away my sins, that you were buried and that You rose from the dead. I ask You to come into my heart, soul, body and mind as my Savior forever.
- I choose to trust You as my Lord and Savior and make you the Head of my life. I ask You to take away my brokenness and make me whole as only You can. I dedicate my life to pleasing You and being the person You created me to be.
- I am standing on Your Word where it says in Matthew 7:7, "Ask and it shall be given you." I have asked and I believe I have received in the Name of my Lord and Savior, Jesus Christ.
- Now Lord fill me with the gift of the Holy Spirit according to Acts 2:38-39 for the promise is unto me and to my children and to all that are far off even as many as the Lord our God shall call.

Contact Prophetess Tyson at
www.prophetessyolandadtyson.com

If you sincerely prayed this prayer, you have just become a child of the Most High God. Congratulations and welcome to the Body of Christ!

Step 3: Use the Promises of God's Word to Stand Against the Enemy

By the Blood of Jesus we have been given authority over all of the power of the enemy. As believers, we can stand on the Word of God as the last word concerning us. It alone is the Truth.

There are three scriptures that speak directly to our power over the enemy. All are found in the New Testament (KJV).

Matthew 10:1

> *And when he had called unto him his twelve disciples, he gave them power against unclean spirits, to cast them out, and to heal all manner of sickness and all manner of disease.*

Matthew 10:7-8

> *[7] And as ye go, preach, saying, the kingdom of heaven is at hand.*
> *[8] Heal the sick, cleanse the lepers, raise the dead, cast out devils: freely ye have received, freely give.*

Luke 10:18-19 (KJV)

84

¹⁸ *And he said unto them, I beheld Satan as lightning fall from heaven.¹⁹ Behold, I give unto you power to tread on serpents and scorpions, and over all the power of the enemy: and nothing shall by any means hurt you.*

These are powerful scriptures to stand on in your deliverance. They hold the promises of God concerning you and your freedom from bondage to the spirit of rejection. Pay attention to them and pray them frequently to remind your spirit man of your position in Christ.

PRAY THIS PRAYER OUT LOUD:

- Father, in the Name of Jesus, I claim the promises of Matthew 10:1, Matthew 10:7-8 and Luke 10:18-19. By the power given to me in Your Word, I take authority over spiritual forces of wickedness that seek to destroy me. I declare and decree that as You said in Isaiah 54:17, no weapon that is formed against me shall prosper. This applies to any and everything that is not of You, including the spirit of rejection and all demonic and unclean spirits that have attached themselves to me. I speak directly to all of you now. In the Name of Jesus and by His blood, I command you to loose me. I bind all of you with the blood of Jesus and command you to go back to dry places. I command you to go back to hell in the Name of the Lord Jesus Christ, out of me and out of this territory never to return. I claim the territory of my mind, my soul, my spirit, my body and my life for the Kingdom of

85

God. You are not welcome here and I resist you with the Word of God and you must flee from me now!

- By the Name and Blood of Jesus, I bind up any opening that I allowed you to come in through.
- I declare that you are not welcome in my life any longer and I cancel any invitation that I may have allowed or sanctioned.
- I cancel any association or connection to any generational curses of rejection and _____ that I adopted through my family lineage.
- I cancel any words of rejection and other curses that were spoken over me at any time from my conception to this moment.
- I cancel the assignment of the enemy through the spirit of rejection and other accompanying spirits that have attached themselves to me, my family, my spouse and my children in the Name of Jesus. I declare the Blood of Jesus is against you and you shall not prosper.
- In the Name of Jesus and by His Blood, I yield myself to the saving grace of Jesus Christ. I give You free reign to heal any wounds whatever their source. I give You freedom to heal every aspect of my life and I withhold nothing from You.
- I confess that I am powerless to heal myself and only Your healing is perfect and complete. In the Name of Jesus and by His blood, I heal, seal and permanently close the wounds of rejection on every level and dimension of my being. I declare that I am a new creature in Christ. Old

Contact Prophetess Tyson at
www.prophetessyolandadtyson.com

things and ways of rejection have passed away. I declare and decree that I am no longer bound by the spirit of rejection or any other associated spirit, in the Name of Jesus.

- I completely yield my mind to You, Jesus. Your Word says to let this mind be in you which was also in Christ Jesus as according to Philippians 2:5. I therefore cancel every thought, belief or imagination that has its source in the spirit of rejection. I choose instead to keep my mind stayed on thee and you keep me in perfect peace (Isaiah 26:3).

- Jesus I thank You and I praise You for the angels You have dispatched in my behalf and that are encamped around me to keep me safe from all attack of the evil one as according to Psalm 34:3.

- I thank You that according to Your Word in Romans 3:22, I am the righteousness of God in Christ Jesus and I am far from oppression of the spirit of rejection in the Name of Jesus.

- I now release power and love in the Holy Ghost, in Jesus' name

Be aware that the enemy will never give up his territory willingly. He may be kicking and screaming by this point. He thinks you are not strong enough to stand against him. You can do all things through Christ which strengthens you (Philippians 4:13)! God is strong enough through you to overcome the enemy. Where you are weak, He is strong! Stand steadfast, unmovable in your confession of faith (Hebrews10:23! Resist

Contact Prophetess Tyson at
www.prophetessyolandadtyson.com

the devil with God's Word and he MUST flee from you (James 4:7)!

Speak to your situation and put the spirit of rejection and any other demonic entity on notice. Their time has passed and they must vacate the premises.

Say the following out loud, like you mean it!

"I claim Jesus, the ruler of all nations in heaven and earth to be the ONLY Lord of my life. Any spirit not like Him and not from Him, I command you to leave now! I command you to leave my body, my mind, my spirit, my home, my family, my pets, my workplace, my vehicle, my finances, and all other areas concerning me! I bind you now, in the Name of Jesus! The Blood is against you! Leave now!

I claim absolute and total authority over you in the Name of Jesus. And I send you back to dry places. According to Philippians 2:9, The Name of Jesus is above every name and you must come subject to it. I command you to do so quickly. In the Name of Jesus, I bind you with the Blood of Jesus and cast you back to dry places. I am redeemed of the Lord. I have been set free. And whom the son sets free is free indeed (John8:36)! Praise God for my freedom in Christ! Thank you Jesus!"

I am a witness that if you follow these steps, you *shall* know the freedom of Christ from the spirit of rejection. Believe it and receive. In my thirty-plus years of ministering deliverance to people all over the country, I know these steps work. I am a living witness. To set the captives free is the gift

88

God has called me to in the kingdom. Determine in your heart today that you are free from bondage and that you will dwell in the House of the Lord forever. If you don't have a church home find, a bible based church and become a part of that church. Amen!

Your work now is to strengthen your walk with God. Study His Word, increase your faith and build your relationship with Him. Really know Him as the God of your salvation and ask Him to continue to show you who you are to Him. Fall in love with Him as He is with you.

Contact Prophetess Tyson at
www.prophetessyolandadtyson.com

Made in the USA
Charleston, SC
10 September 2016